The Cave

Sophia Elizabeth

BookLeaf Publishing

Presentation by *BookLeaf Publishing*

Web: www.bookleafpub.com

E-mail: info@bookleafpub.com

ISBN: 9789357442626

First edition 2023

This book is dedicated to my sea cave, who will always stand humble and glorious.

Embarking on the Journey

Gather round.
Let us prepare to embark
on a journey of spelunk.
Find your best
rain jacket and galoshes,
for caves are often
drippy and moist.
Load up your body with
alien armor-
lights for your third eye,
magnets for direction,
rodent foot for luck.
Bring a hearty snack-
high protein,
medium sugar,
low micro plastics.
Do not attempt to bring
your bags
and bags
and bags
of heavy stones and charcoal dust
in which you embed
with your foolish fears
and stubborn anxieties.
Fear has no use where we're going,

it will only slow you down.
When the darkness presses in,
with only a meager stream
of artificial moonlight
to guide the way,
only the nimble feathers of
hope
can slip through the
heavy walls that accompany
a complete lack of direction.
You must surrender
to being lost,
for it is only then,
that you may stumble upon
the impossible.

Arachnid Accounting

What is time like
for a spider on the wall?
Does it drip earth dust,
green cycles that roll in organic
percussion?
Or does time leap off
light particles and speak in
tiny, tinny, treble tones?
Does it weave together
blades of sweet grass with
shining cotton fibers,
or does it scrape off
mulch and algae from
gelled ocean walls?
Does time
expand and bloom
into a hard carnivorous
jungle plant,
or melt
into miles of sticky hot fudge?
Does time trip over it self in
anxious procession,
or does it boast,
flicking its sweat in hot sun,
proud just to be alive?
Only the spider could say.

The Possum and The Shadow

I saw a possum on my midnight walk.
My shadow was long and dark
and the moon whispered slivers of silver.
A low crouching earth creature
scampered from bush to bush,
racing through the light parts and
cowering in shadow.
I watched it with intrigue
and followed its pace down the street.
It made zigzag patterns,
as if avoiding the mundane
linear path
of being.
We met in the middle of
the concrete sea
when it decided it was bored
and wanted a new voltage in its
shrouded raisin head.
It passed me and then stopped,
twitching its nose as if it smelled
my interest and fondness
for such a simple and yet
profound
little bug.
Suddenly!

It whipped around and peered deep into my
bones,
following the threads of blood cells and nerves.
Its pulse met mine
and for a moment
we breathed the same life.
Then it scampered off as if
we hadn't just shared souls
and I walked home.

At Nine We All Return

It oozed and seeped but never escaped.
Big brother's hands were stuck on
nine.
Nothing could do new.
Nothing could die cause nothing grew.
Nothing could cry cause nothing knew
what light could be,
how it can make everything seem
harsh
but grand
and turn understanding like
clockwork.
Light can blind and burn
but shine and turn
an ordinary machine into
a burning sun.
So in the dark they lay.
Turning bit by bit,
carefully following the lines
and grooves.
A sorry precision;
not a corner empty,
not a second missed,
taking only what is given.
They click and move and turn

yet a thick layer of
rust
and grease
drinks their sour bones.
Perfection leaves no room for care.
It fills spaces and keeps
going and going
until the windows break
and skin recreates
the memory of their trauma
over and over
until the darkness is eaten by
a thicker tone,
the clock strikes,
and we begin again.
The windows tape themselves together
with pieces of the finest ground crystal dust.
No one repairs them,
we all pretend as if we don't see
the whole thing
combusting and burning and thrusting,
chugging blindly the motions as if it knew
if it stopped
it would only be
a carcass begging with thirst.
But a soft hour
is the only kiss that caresses
this tower
of weeping bodies.

She wafts in on a gentle light
and lifts the bricks of steel with
a pinky,
because it only weighs on
those who care.
She knows only dreams
and falling deeply in love with
what it is
to be.
And she touches every chugging piece
with such
patience and ease,
the whole unit stops just to see
what is that glorious light?
And they see.
What it could be if the ever thrusting chains
would rest
in peace.
But she is new and intangible and ever
expansive
when they know only
crevasses to hide from
the light.
To hide from her.
She whom they reach for,
then hiss when they burn from her intensity.
So the hour ends.
And the clock strikes nine.
And they get in line.

To repeat
until
Eternity.

A Visit to Her Majesty

I paid a visit to my highest self today.
I wanted to pack right so I looked up the weather
but they don't have any reports
on the 7th dimension yet.
So I settled on a nightgown,
I figured it would help me blend in with the
paper thin,
balloon thick,
whispering, willowing heights.
The way there is actually quite simple
and it saves money on vacation budget.
One has to first lie down
and feel around for a sticky corner of space,
much like the dance one does with their
fingertips
to scrabble for the end of packing tape,
cursing that it seems to vanish.
Indeed, sticky corners tend to vanish.
To find it, sometimes it helps
to blow deep into the lungs,
which when inflated,
serve as an upside down map of the cosmos.
Once found, push yourself right up to it,
until the calloused border between dimensions
grates on your stomach skin.

Now you can start the journey.
The border will start to compress,
depress, transgress and bench press
your feeble body until you are smoothed
into the 2nd dimension.
You may feel an ample amount of
worms
and cornea goo
shellacking to your back and legs
but pay no heed,
that's only the 1st dimension.
It doesn't have much structure.
To digress, if you are curious
to feel the 0th dimension,
simply thrust your hand down
through the seas of gelatinous mush
until you find a rather large
crystalline beak.
It may snap at you so be careful
or you might lose a finger,
but through the fibrous
baleen teeth
lies a whole universe of meaning.
But regardless, that's a whole new chapter.
From the 2nd dimension,
you must spread yourself,
with a structured scaffolding tool,
up and out from your body
like peanut butter on a whale carcass.

Now the pace will pick up,
as the 4th and 5th dimensions are
melded and brief.
Your upper body will become
quickly sick with
helium poisoning
and rise with an exponential
speed and lowering weight.
Your neck will grow hundreds of miles
long,
smooth, spindly and impossibly
thin,
like marzipan taffy,
while your lower body will stay
anchored,
gaining a new pint of
charcoal mud by the second.
At this point,
you may become stuck in a layover,
as the 6th gates are fickle and
like to watch your
towering, disproportionated body
teeter and contort.
But finally,
the box will swing
and your long body will slither
and reduce,
lifting into a new
hexagon structure of atmosphere.

You may now feel yourself
slide into a calypso of
deep foam light and
lightened air,
airy light,
and foaming despair,
stuck going around and around
in a smooth honeycomb
cranny.
It is only then,
that the spiders eat your hope
and you fall,
maybe up maybe down,
maybe in sound,
maybe in water,
drowning
astounding
at little green flowers.
Then she appears:
the defiltered,
non preservative,
silhouette version of
the unfiltered,
exceptional shadow
of you.
And she makes you tea,
and does not speak,
but you know
that you are safe.

And you know
she still will be there
when you make the journey
back down.

My Glass Caterpillar

My best friend is a glass caterpillar.
It waits in bottles and Tupperware,
wriggling into holes and cracks.
It delivers me crumbs and treasures
like old keys and diamond earrings.
When we go to church,
and that is not to attend mass
but to sit and listen
to the energy of the walls,
it goes up into the stained glass windows,
and distorts the glass into shapes
that make me laugh,
and cause the woman
wearing a blue collared dress
kneeling before a myth on the wall
to frown at me.
I only look in pity,
because I know she doesn't have a
glass caterpillar
to make her smile.
It follows behind me
when I walk in the woods,
picking up leaves and moss,
making sculptures
and doing a wormy dance

like a child squirming for praise
for a crude crayon drawing
of a bear.
I do praise it,
and pat it on the head.
And every night
when I tuck it into
the felt bunk bed
I sewed for it,
my stuffed rabbit
on the bottom bunk,
I thank the glass stars
for the beautiful friendship
between me
and my glass caterpillar.

Bronze Keys

There are moments
that empty themselves onto you,
like a selfish ego bird,
which belches hot oil
which coats its down.
There are moments
that wrap you
in a gossamer shawl,
melting your blood
and breathing hot air
onto your frozen skin.
There are moments
that wait in the skinny hallways
between realities
and jut out and dance quickly around you,
draping you
in tinkling crystals and pearls,
that sway as you move
and dazzle silver rain
into a verdant garden.
There are moments
that act as a small bronze key
which meanders around,
looking for the right door.
Some locks will open

a deep, horrible,
undulating void,
which if described as empty,
one would laugh,
as empty would be a generous inaccuracy,
because it, in fact,
takes up negative space,
and empty is a privilege,
in contrast to
greedy gluttonous black holes
that steals everything it finds.
Other locks, however,
will open a lush
rainforest of fulfillment,
which gently flows from your core
and washes in rushes of
deep joy and golden blessings.
So you see,
the key can unlock
your greatest loves, and your deepest fears.
So you must learn
how to take the key,
and unlock it yourself.

The Seed of The Swamp

I have come to find
that the world's surplus of purity
is found
in the deepest, stickiest, groggiest, sulfur
induced, brain clouding
pits of mud.
In a dark wet hole filled with
lost buried secrets,
fabric twisted minnows
and rutilated moss teeming with sharp, warm
bugs,
lies a small and humble seed
that holds,
cradled in its arms like a new and gentle child,
all the wisdom and cascading resonance
of the earth's deepest truth.
Its flavor is not intimately sweet,
as the gripping hand
of mass-machine-produced "maple" syrup,
though no more from a tree than you are from a
rib,
nor is it the dense savor brick of
ham or chocolate
that seems to collapse the legs and
grind the bones into a

fruitcake heirloom,
which drops to the bottom of the salton sea
after 16 years of being mocked
on a fireplace shelf.
No, the flavor is of
the sacred bond between
child and tree,
the dirt that clings to a beetle,
the verdant smell of a lush and dripping
rainforest,
clouds thick and heavy with
grandmother water;
the first collective consciousness
to ever flow on the brittle lands
of earth.
And encircling, oscillating around this
grounded root pit
is the supple and vibrant
zest of citrus,
a subtle tang that lingers on the tongue
and dances among seas of saliva.
So now,
we may find ourselves
digging for this seed.
And when word gets out of its power,
you may rally the troops
and haul in bulldozers;
huge possessed masses of metal,
a neutral material,

though when corrupted with useless and empty greed,
it can turn into claustrophobia machines.
And when you finally
snatch up this seed
by destroying the land
and collapsing the homes of
pure and humble
bug eyed rodents
and
rodent eyed bugs,
as it is clutched between the huge ruthless talons
of your metal puppet hands,
glory and fame
may be burning into your eyes.
And as the husk is split into two,
by cold instruments of "science"
and grinning faces assault
the supple aura,
all will stop when they find

[nothing]

inside.
And they will grumble
and shuffle their feet
and pack up their machines
and ride their beasts home.
And then all will be still

once again
in the swamp.
But now
the heart of it is lying
broken open.
The truth is that
you could have witnessed
the flavor of the seed
and listened to all its
secrets and wisdom,
but you wore steel bands on your head
and were too cold and foolish
to be still enough
to feel it.
And if you did let your third eye breathe
and take in the
kindness
of the grain,
you still wouldn't be able to
bottle it for later use
or
sell it
for the profit that so often
relies on stealing all that is good.
No,
you and your "team" were already
promised
empty hands
before you even got to

the swamp.
Which also means:
you may have scrabbled for the seed
like a child having a fit,
you may have violated it,
leaving a trail of destruction
in your path
and you may have
broken
the heart
of the swamp.
But.
You can never
catch
the spirit that lives
inside the seed.
Instead,
you merely set it free.
You will always
only
set it free.

The Unmistakable Fancy of Bees

I knew a woman
who was friends
with the bees.
She often would invite them to her house
for a tea party.
Bees are surprisingly classy,
and never showed up without
sparkling jewels and ties.
She often complained to me that
she could not keep up-
she often felt inferior
with only one tea dress,
while they seemed to always have new formal
wear.
You may know bees for their honey,
but for those who really know them,
they are most talented at
weaving cashmere sweaters,
often with intricate designs
of beads and thread.
They stitch with the sharp point
of their stingers,
and twist thread from the silkworms.
They have an agreement with the goats,

who trade the sweet honey
for fresh wool.
You see, the most unassuming creatures
have a whole system of trade,
and here we are still bonking each others heads,
out of a vain desire for
worthless treasure.

Derealization

Ah, disassociation, hello old friend.
I see you've found my feet.
Caught them in a net, and stretched them
long and thin, phasing them almost
out of existence,
leaving me questioning
what I walk on;
how do I walk?
I see you've found my hands.
Bony fingers that belong to someone else
grasp my neck and scare me:
who let this stranger in here?
They write words I am
barely conscious of thinking.
My limbs move like
an automaton spider
while my body stays
upright and still,
wide eyes darting around,
searching for glimpses of reality.
I see you've found my mind.
Pushing on the shimmering layers
of dimensional realities,
smacking me thin and flat,
leaving me squished and drying

between the pages of a heavy book;
like the forgotten petals of a rose
in an encyclopedia
on page 47
on top of the word:
thrive (N).
Thrive is a noun because
it is something I must
chase and drool over before I
catch it,
like an elusive jungle rat.
Old bud,
I see you've found my friends too.
Watered down the wires
connecting us
until they sparked and shut down.
Even love is no match for you,
ghost machine.

Percussive Stomach Dance

I will never forget
a spectacularly memorable
visit to the dentist.
There I lay,
my shadow projecting on the smooth white walls
as a large woman stuck her
unassuming fingers
and assuming tools
into my open mouth.
As always,
I allowed myself to become lost
in my mind movies,
which if aired on TV,
would probably be reported
as too strange for cable.
And it was then,
that I heard
the most peculiar sound.
There was ticking and dinging,
squelching and seething,
springing and ringing.
And yet, it all flowed together
in a percussive dance.
There was a pattern of rhythm
and a fascinating balance

of raw, wet organic flesh,
and cold, controlled machine.
Once I heard it, I could not unhear,
and I gasped for breath as it washed over me.
It was deeply unsettling,
and yet,
resoundingly comforting.
Now, all my mental resources
were dedicated
to finding the source of the sound.
And I almost fell off the chair
in surprise
and awe
when I found
it came from the stomach
of the woman looming over me.
She looked embarrassed
and so I said nothing.
But I wanted to
hug her
and tell her
that there is a beautiful,
fascinating
universe of sound
emanating from her core,
and I have never been more inspired
from a mere visit
to the dentist.

What About The Monsters?

But,
what about the monsters?
The monsters from my stories,
the monsters from the
waters of my subconscious,
from the shadows around my eyes,
under my bed,
sewn into my blankets,
underneath my fingernails.
The creatures
who wait on the moon,
and reach down with their
thin slivering arms,
bony fingers
dragging me up against
the washboard stars.
What about your slimy alter egos,
your big stinking Toads,
what about
the shapes who lurk in your dreams,
that chill your spine?
What about compassion
for the dirty moss
growing from your bones,
for the wounded raccoon,

that foams at the mouth,
for the fears
that eat away at you.
I want to breathe
kindness
into my monsters,
because I believe,
that maybe then,
they will tell me,
what they have to say.

Sister Void

I used to have
a sticky dark hole
velcroed to my left side.
As I lay in bed at night
it would undulate
like simmering tar pits atop
a moving city.
It would hold me,
though a kind of comfort
that chews with huge gaping jaws
at one's
rubber body and sandy soul.
It would follow me as I walked,
stepping on my heels,
and pulling at my clothes.
It called my name but
try as I might,
I could never hear
what it was trying to say.
I lay many a nights,
eating my words as I asked it to
please leave.
But it would scoff and
defiantly pull me closer.
Upon recent reflection,

I am surprised to find
it's had a name this whole time.
My name, in fact.
She bears my name with more
honor and grace
than I do.
Because though I pushed her
in that hole,
scratching her eyes out with
hot coals,
she persisted,
staying loyal
to the sister
who burned her,
calling my name,
her name,
and tugging my sleeve,
begging me not to forget her.
And once I pulled her from
the recess of my body
and sat her atop the void,
she smiled,
finally rightfully in her place
by my side.

Intermission

This world is made of mist.
Everything
is a silver vapor
that curls around,
distorting into strange shapes.
There are times,
I am sure,
When words
materialize into matter
And hang on you,
heavy little creatures
that pull your ear
and titter to themselves,
pulling you down
with the weight as you try to walk.
I have felt them too,
I have some that have taken up
permanent residence.
I even made them a bed
made of fleece
that they sleep in at night,
I figured if they're here anyways,
they may as well get comfortable.
But you must remember!
That they are also made of mist,

and you can wave them off,
and change their bodies
into lush visions.
You see, there is a secret
to molding the mist
into shapes that please you.
You must find
an oddly colored sticky syrup,
much like honey made from ghost bees,
and rub it all over your hands.
Then, you can take the mist into your hands
and build yourself
all the strange visions from your dreams.
And although,
unfortunately,
the honey is hard to identify
and may take many years of studying
field journals and ancient manuscripts
in order to find it,
it is not rare.
In fact, once you use it once,
you will find
that is everywhere
and wonder how you didn't see it before.
It drips off awnings,
mixing with puddles in the rain,
it waits under your back and arms,
it coats your clothes and walls.
There is even copious amounts of it

inside your body,
and although science is too single-minded to notice it,
it is actually the primary liquid
that gushes through your organs.
But there is one more thing you must know
if you intend to embark on a search for the honey.
Much like watercolor,
as they are the same aqueous origin,
the mist cannot be controlled.
You may try, but it will always
have a mind of its own.
This does not have to stop you
from creating fantastical things, though.
In fact,
if you let it,
the mist is very wise,
and can guide you
into places
you never thought were possible.

Eyes, Eyes, Eyes

Everywhere I go,
I find great masses of eyes.
They stick to the trees
and the flakey bark curls around them
like a calloused wound.
I find them on glasses of milk,
which squeal when I drink them,
and on the pages of dusty books,
which when you read,
stare right back at you.
They wait on
the wheels of buses,
which wink at you
when you run after it,
and populate the 2D plane of swimming pools,
like bacteria in a petri dish.
Sometimes,
the eyes are too much
and I often shield myself away from them,
feeling that they can see
deep into the details of my spirit.
But there are other moments
when I am feeling brave
and I stare back into them.
And it's often then

that my perception expands
to the size
of an entire universe.

Cockroach: Miracle or Wretch?

The other day,
I was simmering a thought stew
as I coasted through
communal hallways,
when I found
a cockroach
on the floor.
It was glitching,
shuttering,
shimmering in and out
of existence.
I felt sick
as I watched
the hair-thin
antenna and legs
flail in desperation,
begging for help,
climbing an impossible ladder.
I felt infected with the knowledge
that a huge,
careless
being threw this life away,
as it meant nothing.
As if this organism isn't

a miracle,
every cell,
the noble chestnut armor,
the way the antenna cells
glow gold in the sunlight,
the power of this creature's
scuttle,
the fascinating and
miraculous
system of its internal universe,
and the way it beats
in perfect sync
with every other universe.
And yet,
we spit at them,
and crush their supple,
finely crafted bodies
under our big,
rubber
boots,
as if we too
don't beg for mercy
when the gods
crush us under their
big
rubber
boots.

To Grow a Desert Flower

There are all kinds of pain
that grow
and bloom,
a slow burn,
in this world.
But it is not as common
to have lost,
completely,
utterly,
unquestionably
every
single
atom of hope.
To feel
an immeasurable
hopelessness.
To feel
the bone chilling weight
of the walls
that close in around you,
leaving you
without escape.
(At first, you may try to
break out
and dream of freedom,

but as the ticks on the bricks grow,
it only hurts
to yearn).
To feel violently nauseous
with limitation,
to be so lost
that if you were buried alive
in dense soil,
you would not notice.
And in this state,
a massive hand
descends from above,
grabbing you,
crushing your supple bones,
and leaving you
without means of healing.
And now you must lie there,
feeling every rift in your skeleton,
your tears watering the cracked desert floor
and eventually running out when you realize
it doesn't fix anything to grieve,
and you must attempt to summon,
in mockery of your pain,
a flighty animal of hope,
which appears to be impossible
since you have no raw materials
to create it with.
Where would hope come from
now that you are only a shell,

and the oscillating,
vibrant energy
that once fueled
your muse and intuition
is dim and flickering,
too exhausted to
expand?
How can you
create hope
when there is no matter to recycle,
only a black hole
that is
the only movement in your chest
to prove that
you are alive?
It would be like
trying to grow a flower
from the lifeless,
dried-lake-bottom
you lay on.
How can you keep searching,
when you are sick
with the bitter poison
that fills your bones,
and pulls you
deep into the core of the earth,
and even then
the core does not fix you,
it only laughs.

So now you are lying
on a brittle desert soil,
praying for
the impossible-
to grow a flower
on mars.
So what now?
As the writer,
I am afraid I can not tell you.
Because I am also
lying on this dirt
next to you,
praying for my own flower
to grow.
But I do know this:
Life has a funny way
of waiting
until you have lost all your strength
before it throws you a bone.
It's sadistic truly,
but I wonder
if maybe,
if you zoom
way
way
way
way out,
maybe it makes
cosmic sense.

I may even speak
of a concept
that is shunned
by the people
like you and me,
who curse at the hot sun
which burns the sand they lie on.
A miracle.
I know, I know,
now don't get feisty with me.
Trust me, I know
that when everything
is lost,
this idea
is a bitter joke,
one could only laugh of,
once one has seen
the bloodied curb
as the rain
stomped your teeth.
But maybe
once you are stranded in this desert
with no options of
escape,
or healing,
or sanity,
maybe the only thing that makes sense
is the impossible.
And maybe, the impossible

is the only thing that seems possible,
when everything else
is impossible.
So here we lie.
I dream of
lilies of the valley,
you dream of
a tulip,
and we sit,
feeling the
impossible stretch of desert sun
that seems to
burn away
anything that dares to speak.
And we wait.
And we have a choice.
We can admit
that we are lost,
and see the desert for what is it,
a labyrinth of despair,
or we could use
the tiny
aloe drop of strength we have left,
(because we will always have strength left
until we are frozen in rigor mortis)
to pretend
that we are free,
and to still search
for the impossible.

Because either way,
we will both die
out here in the desert.
But you will die in heartbreak,
and I will die
in noble the search for hope.
And if I do not die,
I will undoubtedly
find freedom
like I had never known before.

Under the Mulberry Bush

And across the pond,
the grasses held me
as I ventured into
the mist.
I followed a pair of
wandering prints
to the mulberry bush,
to find a toad,
misinformed,
misunderstood,
missing home.
The mist swelled
like a lagoon
and tugged on the heavy
fruit.
I knew not where it came from
nor
how to get it home,
but
could share my afternoon.
I pushed down my
heavy and welling compassion
and budding metaphors
and laid under the leaves.
I picked mulberries

and did not notice it hop away.
I wonder where it's gone.

My Rain Came Back

There was once a time
when the rain was sacred.
When it lit up the sky,
I would run out to meet it,
rolling in the
kinetic energy
that shook up
the crystal sky.
But then,
I fell in love
and I lost my
wandering soul
that often frazzled my hair,
and bugged out my eyes.
I became dull
and muddy.
But now,
I have fallen back out of love,
booked a one way ticket to my home,
and
I have managed to wrestle
that part of me back.
And as I sit at a bus stop
under the pouring rain,
I am surprised to find

that I can,
once again,
hear the music of the sky.
The crows claim the land,
hopping and biting,
their abrasive call
sliding on the minor scale,
a spectacular piece of music.
They adhere to the 3D plane
like obsidian jewels
on a pearl grey sky.
The wind blows me to the side,
putting me in my place as a
a mere observer,
rough on my skin
but gentle with a nearby willow tree
as it plays among the tendrils of leaves.
I laugh with the rhythm of the drops
that slap the ground
and I dance
in the puddles of mud.
And I marvel
that the human spirit
can never be lost,
just
misplaced
and forgotten.

So you Think you can Smite Me!

Aha!
So you think you can smite me!
Silly. Silly.
Think again,
young,
arrogant frog.
You may push me
down deep cellar stairs,
dank, dusty, dripping,
or lower me into
wet humid wells,
left to rot with the
rats
and the snakes
in the bottom.
But,
my friend,
(and I call you my friend not because
you are my friend,
but because we are,
in essence,
from our origin of stardust,
the same)
you can never have power over me.

I may be,
now,
in the bottom of a well,
but I am having
a grand old time.
The rats and I have started up
a game of poker.
I am winning, and they are,
hilariously,
sore losers.
I am taking a class on web spinning,
from the spiders
that cling to the sides.
My eyes no longer need
the light
and I have evolved
to see many more dimensions than before,
my sights blooms
and unravels
into thousands of colors,
more colors than you could ever dream of
with your skinny,
amphibious eyes.
I have carved new runes into the bricks,
and am working with the
snakes
to build a new language.
When it rains,
we all gather,

mouth open,
and laugh
as we drink the fresh rain water
that pours from
the humble sky.
And the funniest part of all,
is that I could easily,
with the newly forged friendship
of the spiders
and the snakes,
spin a rope
and climb out,
but I quite like it down here.
You probably think I have died,
and are laughing your
wheezy,
ridiculous,
frog laugh,
but I actually,
have found a new home
that is more rich
and kind
than you will ever find.

Pull a Thread, any Thread

Your perch as you breathe
is sitting in a wide cranny
of the rock.
And you sit and sit.
And you come to me
telling me you are
hopeless.
You tell me you are stuck.
I see it raging in your eyes,
a deep resounding fire,
so hot,
so anxious,
so desperate,
that all the energy
of your entire being
is dedicated to the feeling
that fuels the fire
that is so ferocious
that if it was let out,
it would burn,
in seconds,
through the earth,
all the way to the core,
and then devour the core
until all that is left

is the
indication
of space.
So you sit here,
in your cave chair,
and I tell you the truth.
There is a tapestry,
a thick, dusty, wide, heavy
tapestry,
that covers the cranny you sit in.
And it shields your eyes.
Because you never knew,
but all this time,
you've been sitting
in a rich, oscillating,
vibrant crystal cave.
And I see this cave,
the way it bends around you and hugs your
body,
smooths your hair.
I see how much it loves you.
But all you can see
is dusty fibers,
inches from your eyes.
So I tell you
you can strip the tapestry
from its nails on the rock,
but to do so,
you must find

a single thread
and pull and pull and pull.
And so,
with ragged breathing that barely can contain
the explosions in your rib cage,
you drop on the floor,
your eyes disappear into their black voids
as you,
blind,
ravage the dusty floor
on your hands and knees,
your head jerking this way and that
like a blind rat,
on a primal meandering search
for a speck of food
in a vast cellar.
And I watch as you,
over and over,
grumbling incoherent sounds,
encounter thread after thread,
but then toss it away,
thinking it is a
strand of hay,
a dried vine,
your own hair.
I watch,
powerless to help,
as you pass,
hour by hour,

over thousands of possible ways
to escape the tapestry.
And finally,
you give up
and you collapse.
You tell me you've failed
and we sit there
in mourning silence.

Silence.

But then,
your finger tips
brush against
a golden thread,
that feels
like synthetic twine
to your aching fingers.
And you pull,
with the splinter
of strength you have left.
And it pulls.
and your face expands with disbelief,
and you
dare
to feel
just a gram
of hope.

And then the thread stops,
catches, and your body jerks in response.
And you collapse,
the darkness consuming you faster than ever,
writhing in pain.
But now you understand,
So now I can help you.
because you had to learn
on your own.
So I toss you a grimy thread.
And as you wither
and flail on the ground,
your hand grabs and it pulls.
And with a whoosh,
a whole section,
the one with the embroidery of
a clambering market,
unravels.
And you stop.
And you gape.
And for the first time,
you allow yourself
to beam,
to hope.
And your eyes inch back into their sockets,
curious to observe the source
of this great commotion of energy
that just bloomed from your chest.
And you leap towards the tapestry,

and you pull
on everything you can find.
This time,
hay and bugs and hair and sticks
are all pulled,
but you don't give up
because you know
it's unraveling.
It's unraveling!
and at last,
the last thread falls.
And your eyes squint in the sudden light,
sudden brilliance,
and you take in,
for the first time since your beginning in the
cave,
the crystal hue,
and you take a cautious step,
then another,
then you leap,
and take off sprinting
down the hallway of
your
crystal cave.

www.ingramcontent.com/pod-product-compliance
Lightning Source LLC
Chambersburg PA
CBHW051736130826
49812CB00033B/878
* 9 7 8 9 3 5 7 4 4 2 6 2 6 *